NELSON MANDELA

ODYSSEYS

VALERIE BODDEN

CREATIVE EDUCATION · CREATIVE PAPERBACKS

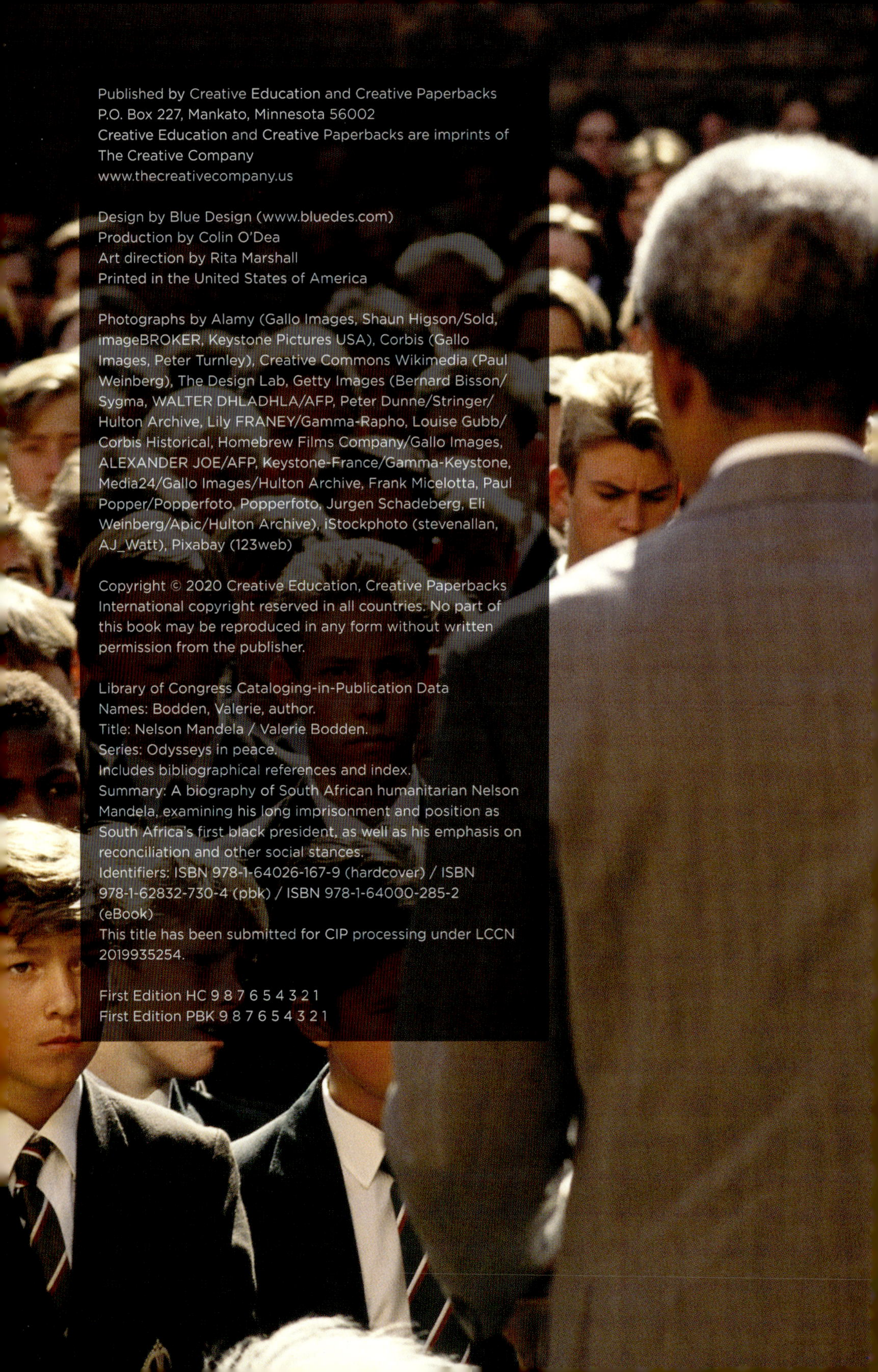

Published by Creative Education and Creative Paperbacks
P.O. Box 227, Mankato, Minnesota 56002
Creative Education and Creative Paperbacks are imprints of The Creative Company
www.thecreativecompany.us

Design by Blue Design (www.bluedes.com)
Production by Colin O'Dea
Art direction by Rita Marshall
Printed in the United States of America

Photographs by Alamy (Gallo Images, Shaun Higson/Sold, imageBROKER, Keystone Pictures USA), Corbis (Gallo Images, Peter Turnley), Creative Commons Wikimedia (Paul Weinberg), The Design Lab, Getty Images (Bernard Bisson/Sygma, WALTER DHLADHLA/AFP, Peter Dunne/Stringer/Hulton Archive, Lily FRANEY/Gamma-Rapho, Louise Gubb/Corbis Historical, Homebrew Films Company/Gallo Images, ALEXANDER JOE/AFP, Keystone-France/Gamma-Keystone, Media24/Gallo Images/Hulton Archive, Frank Micelotta, Paul Popper/Popperfoto, Popperfoto, Jurgen Schadeberg, Eli Weinberg/Apic/Hulton Archive), iStockphoto (stevenallan, AJ_Watt), Pixabay (123web)

Library of Congress Cataloging-in-Publication Data
Names: Bodden, Valerie, author.
Title: Nelson Mandela / Valerie Bodden.
Series: Odysseys in peace.
Includes bibliographical references and index.
Summary: A biography of South African humanitarian Nelson Mandela, examining his long imprisonment and position as South Africa's first black president, as well as his emphasis on reconciliation and other social stances.
Identifiers: ISBN 978-1-64026-167-9 (hardcover) / ISBN 978-1-62832-730-4 (pbk) / ISBN 978-1-64000-285-2 (eBook)
This title has been submitted for CIP processing under LCCN 2019935254.

First Edition HC 9 8 7 6 5 4 3 2 1
First Edition PBK 9 8 7 6 5 4 3 2 1

NELSON MANDELA

NELSON
MANDELA
LEADER OF

CONTENTS

Introduction

When Nelson Mandela emerged from prison on February 11, 1990, no one was sure what to expect. The South African freedom fighter had been jailed for 26 years. The country's **apartheid** government had banned his image, so the last picture the world had seen of him was from before he went to prison in 1964, at the age of 46. Now 71, the man who walked out the prison gates had certainly changed in appearance. Though still tall and dignified, Mandela's silvery hair was evidence of how much time had passed.

OPPOSITE: Within hours of his release from prison, Mandela delivered a 30-minute speech to a crowd of nearly 100,000 that had gathered in front of Cape Town's City Hall.

OPPOSITE In the weeks leading up to South Africa's historic 1994 elections, thousands of people showed their support for Mandela's candidacy at rallies held by the ANC.

However, the most notable change in the freed man was his view of how to win the struggle for racial equality in his country. Where once he had called for militant resistance, Mandela now called for reconciliation. He expressed his vision that all South Africans, no matter their race, could work together to build their future.

It was a vision some people embraced and others decried. It was a vision he worked toward as the nation's first democratically elected president. And it is a vision for which the people of South Africa continue to strive. As they do, they are guided by the example set by Mandela, whom many acknowledge as one of the greatest humanitarians of all time.

ANC

From African Royal to Freedom Fighter

Rolihlahla Mandela, who would be given the English name Nelson when he began school, was born on July 18, 1918. His birthplace was Mvezo, a small village in the hills of southeastern South Africa. Mandela's family belonged to the royal line of the **Thembu** people, 1 of 12 tribes that make up the **Xhosa** nation.

OPPOSITE: Later on, one of the nicknames ascribed to Mandela was "Madiba," which is also the clan name of the Thembu kings.

Mandela's father, Gadla Henry Mphakanyiswa, had four wives, including Mandela's Mother, Nosekeni Fanny. Of Mandela's 12 siblings, 3 were brothers. Mandela's father served as adviser to the Thembu king. The white government recognized Gadla as a village headman. But only a year after Mandela's birth, Gadla was stripped of his position for refusing to obey an order from local white authorities. Nosekeni moved with her children to Qunu, a slightly larger village about 30 miles (48.3 km) away. Gadla visited once a month.

Mandela later remembered his years in Qunu as the happiest of his childhood. The family lived in three rondavels, or round huts with mud walls and grass roofs. Mandela spent his days looking after the family's sheep and calves in the fields, hunting birds with a slingshot, and

Many Names

Mandela's birth name, Rolihlahla, could be translated as "troublemaker." All African students were also given an English name when they started school. Mandela said this was because "whites were unable or unwilling to pronounce an African name, and considered it uncivilized to have one." His teacher chose the name Nelson for him. When he turned 16, Mandela went through a circumcision ritual to mark his passage to manhood. He was given the circumcision name Dalibunga. Later in life, he was often addressed as Madiba, after the name of his clan within the Thembu people. The use of this name was a sign of respect.

swimming in the clear streams that crisscrossed the area. Stick-fighting was a favorite pastime for the village boys. Mandela later recalled that his days in the village taught him how to defeat opponents without humiliating them.

The South Africa into which Mandela was born was marked by racial divisions. The minority white population was made up mainly of British settlers and Afrikaners—descendants of the Dutch, German, and French settlers who had arrived in South Africa in the 1600s. These whites controlled the government. They denied many rights to the majority black African population.

For example, native Africans were allowed to own land in only 13 percent of the country. Africans had to ride separate buses and attend separate schools—if they went to school at all. Every nonwhite South African had to carry a pass identifying where they were from. But in Qunu, Mandela was relatively sheltered from the effects of these laws. He rarely encountered whites. He believed the few whites he met were "to be treated with a mixture of fear and respect."

When Mandela was 12, his father died. Afterward, Mandela was taken to the Thembu royal palace in Mqhekezweni. There he was raised by the Thembu **regent**, or head chief, Jongintaba Dalindyebo. Mandela attended the local mission school, where he received a British education. But he also learned about leadership as he observed how Jongintaba ruled. He noted that the regent invited all Thembus to important meetings. Everyone was allowed to speak, and the regent listened without interrupting. At the end of the meeting, Jongintaba would try to bring the people to a consensus. Mandela later called this form of governance "the seeds

Not Ready to Fight

While in college, Mandela brought his friend Paul Mahabane home with him for a holiday break. The two young men were near the local post office when they were approached by a local white official. The official told Mahabane to go into the post office and purchase some stamps for him. Mahabane refused. Although Mandela admired his courage, he also admitted he wouldn't have been ready to do the same himself. Still, he said Mahabane's example helped him see "that a black man did not have to accept the dozens of petty indignities directed at him each day."

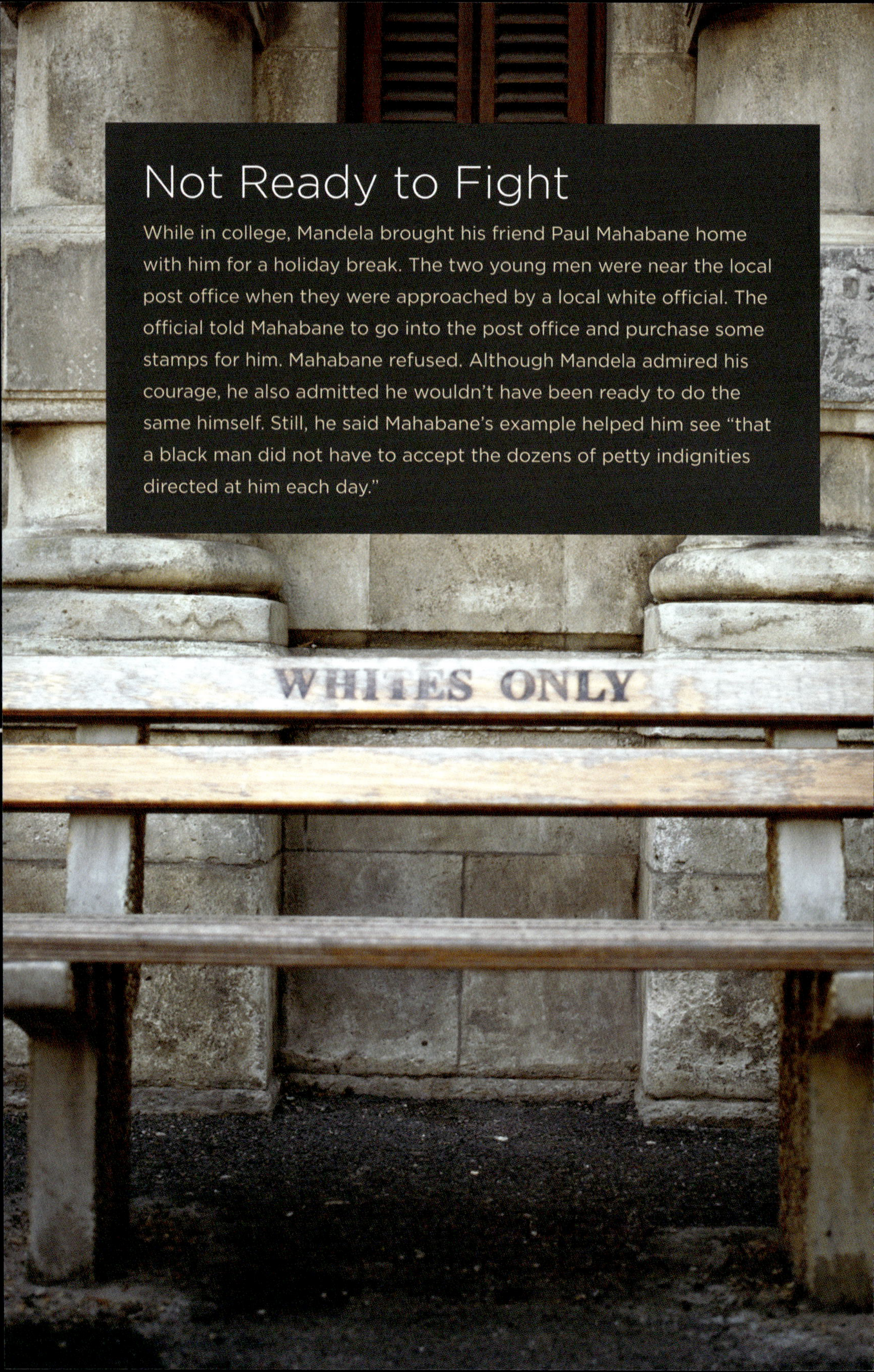

of revolutionary democracy."

Jongintaba groomed Mandela to become the adviser to the next Thembu king. He sent Mandela to Clarkebury Boarding Institute, a secondary (high) school for Africans. Afterward, Mandela went to Healdtown, a large black college. By the time he entered the University College of Fort Hare in 1939, Mandela had decided he no longer wanted to be an adviser to the king. Instead, he wanted to become an interpreter in the government's Native Affairs Department. This position was among the highest a black man could achieve in South Africa at the time. Mandela felt it would give him the prestige and security he sought. Then, with only a year left to obtain his degree, Mandela was expelled for protesting against the school's poor food by refusing to sit on a student council. Soon afterward, Jongintaba announced he had

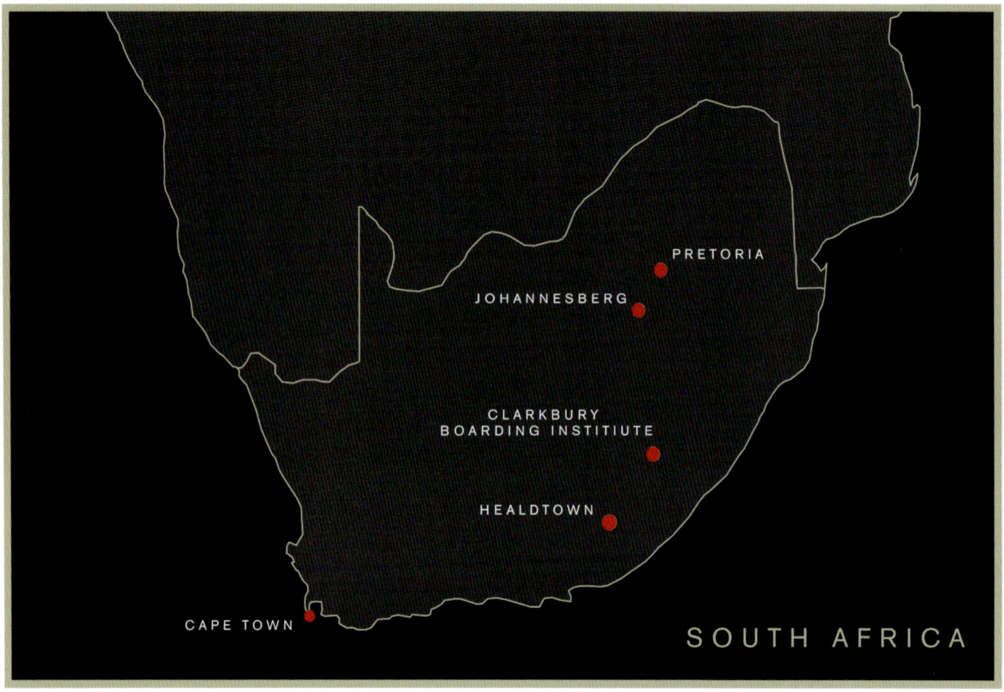

arranged a marriage for Mandela. Unwilling to marry the woman Jongintaba had chosen, Mandela instead fled to Johannesburg, nearly 600 miles (966 km) away.

When he arrived in Johannesburg in 1941, Mandela thought it was "a city of dreams, a place where one could transform oneself." Although he quickly found a job as a clerk in a law firm, his salary was barely enough to keep him fed. He rented a small room in one of the city's many slums, where blacks lived in shacks with no

ATLANTIC OCEAN
SOUTH AFRICA

OPPOSITE Under apartheid, the city of Johannesburg became a juxtaposition of inequality with towering skyscrapers and dilapidated shantytowns.

electricity or indoor plumbing. At night, he studied by candlelight to finish his degree.

Despite the tough conditions, Mandela began to see Johannesburg as home. He made new friends, both black and white. Some of them, including Walter Sisulu, were heavily involved in politics. At their prompting, Mandela joined the African National Congress (ANC), a political party for nonwhite Africans. The organization called on the government to eliminate discriminatory laws and establish a truly democratic government in which all Africans would have equal rights.

Mandela quickly moved up the ranks in the ANC, soon taking a position on the national executive committee. He also started a family, marrying Evelyn Ntoko Mase in 1944. The two eventually had four children together. In addition to his unpaid work for the ANC,

CLEGHORN & HARRIS LTD
ACKS
RYTHING
SICAL
AND
TRICAL
CLEGHORNS
BAZAARS
TEA
STANLEY MOTORS

TAKEAWAY

In 1948, the National Party—led largely by Afrikaners—won control of South Africa's government.

Mandela opened the first black law firm in South Africa with fellow activist **Oliver Tambo**.

In 1948, the National Party—led largely by Afrikaners—won control of South Africa's government. The party quickly established a new system known as apartheid, or "apartness." Under apartheid, all South Africans were classified by race—white, black, Indian, or Coloured (mixed white and black ancestry). Cities were divided into separate areas for each race. No one from another race could live, do business, or own land in the areas set aside for other races.

In response to the new regulations, Mandela led the

ANC in launching the Defiance Campaign on June 26, 1952. Volunteers deliberately broke what they saw as unjust laws. Some traveled into white neighborhoods, while others used "whites-only" facilities. Mandela himself was arrested for breaking curfew, although he was released on bail two days later.

By the end of the Defiance Campaign, Mandela had become nationally known as a leader in the liberation struggle. His growing popularity earned him a banning order from the government. This order prohibited him from traveling outside Johannesburg. He couldn't attend meetings of any kind—not even his children's birthday parties.

During his preparations for the Defiance Campaign, Mandela had emphasized to volunteers that all protests must remain nonviolent. But Mandela never embraced

OPPOSITE After the South African government declared the ANC illegal in 1960, political refugees in Tanzania and elsewhere continued to organize peaceful protests.

nonviolence as an ethical principle. He instead felt nonviolence was a tactic to be used only as long as it was effective. Should it become ineffective, Mandela was willing to turn to more violent forms of protest. "Nonviolent passive resistance is effective as long as your opposition adheres to the same rules as you do," he wrote. "There is no moral goodness in using an ineffective weapon."

QUOTE

"The day of reckoning between the forces of freedom and those of reaction is not very far off.... To overthrow oppression has been sanctioned by humanity and is the highest aspiration of every free man."

- Nelson Mandela, "No Easy Walk to Freedom" speech, 1953

From Nonviolent Activist to Militant Leader

On June 25 and 26, 1955, more than 3,000 members of the ANC and other liberation groups joined in a Congress of the People. The Congress created a Freedom Charter, outlining a vision for the future of the country in which all South Africans would have the right to a free and representative government. Mandela saw the

OPPOSITE: Mandela became interested in South African politics after working as a law clerk; he soon joined forces with Tambo to fight discrimination in the courtroom.

document as both a "blueprint for the liberation struggle" and a work that "captured the hopes and dreams of the people" for a democratic future.

In December 1956, Mandela and 155 other leaders of the liberation movement were arrested on charges of high treason. The state argued that the Freedom Charter was proof of a plan to violently overthrow the government. If convicted, the men could face the death sentence. The case dragged on for nearly five years. For most of that time, the defendants were out on bail, though they had to report to the court in Pretoria nearly every day. Because he was unable to attend to clients, Mandela's law firm crumbled. His marriage also fell apart. He and his wife divorced. Mandela soon remarried. His new wife, Nomzamo Winifred Madikizela, quickly joined him in the liberation struggle. The two eventually had two children together.

The "Treason Trial" finally came to an end on March 29, 1961. The court found Mandela and the others accused not guilty. But Mandela did not return home to celebrate the verdict. Only a year earlier, the South African government had declared the ANC illegal. Instead of closing their doors, however, the organization's leaders had decided to take their work underground. They had already sent Tambo out of the country to set up a new ANC headquarters, which he eventually established in Lusaka, Zambia. Mandela, meanwhile,

TREASON TRIAL
The ACCUSED
DECEMBER 1956

would remain in South Africa, working undercover to keep the ANC going.

As the state became even more ruthless in its hunt for liberation activists, Mandela began a hidden existence. He stayed in empty apartments or in supporters' homes, lying low during the day. When he needed to go out, he did so disguised as a chauffeur, gardener, or chef. At night, he would emerge, seeking to drum up support for the ANC. Mandela knew this life was dangerous—the police had issued a warrant for his arrest—and he missed his family. But, he felt it "was something I knew I had to do.... When a man is denied the right to live the life he believes in, he has no choice but to become an outlaw."

As he met with other ANC leaders, Mandela now tried to convince them of the necessity for militant action. Mandela said they had tried every possible course of nonviolent action and had failed. He said that the government's turn to violence left them no choice but to respond in kind. Not everyone in the ANC agreed. Many felt there were still nonviolent options available to them. But Mandela argued that "it was wrong and immoral to subject our people to armed attacks by the state without offering them some kind of alternative." Other ANC leaders worried that turning to violent methods would only lead to stronger government oppression. Mandela countered that the people were so fed up that violence was going to break out whether the ANC led it or not. He argued that, by leading the violent movement, they could help to direct its outcome.

In the end, Mandela's arguments won out. The ANC authorized him to set up a new, militant branch that would operate separately from the ANC. The new organization was named Umkhonto we Sizwe, or "Spear of the Nation," known as MK for short. Though he had no military training, Mandela was named the organization's chairman. Still working underground, Mandela moved to a small farm in Rivonia, a suburb just north of Johannesburg. There he set up MK headquarters. He and the other leaders of MK decided they would start with acts of sabotage against state targets, such as power plants, telephone lines, and transportation. They hoped such attacks would draw the South African government toward negotiations to make them stop. But if not, Mandela was prepared to lead his organization in acts of terrorism and even **guerrilla** warfare.

On December 16, 1961, MK detonated homemade bombs at power stations and government offices in several cities. They sent out leaflets declaring, "The time comes in the life of any nation when there remain only two choices: submit or fight. That time has now come to South Africa. We shall not submit and we have no choice but to hit back by all means within our power."

As MK continued to carry out sabotage operations, Mandela illegally left South Africa in January 1962. He traveled across Africa, meeting with heads of state in several countries and seeking their support for MK's operations. He also spent two months in a guerrilla training camp in Ethiopia, where he learned to shoot and to make small bombs.

Mandela returned to South Africa in July 1962. On August 5, he was caught and arrested. Found guilty of inciting a strike and of leaving the country without a passport, he was sentenced to five years in prison. Less than a year into his prison term, however, Mandela was

TAKEAWAY

Mandela returned to South Africa in July 1962. On August 5, he was caught and arrested.

summoned back to court.

The South African police had raided MK headquarters at Rivonia, confiscating hundreds of incriminating documents. Mandela, Sisulu, and other MK leaders were charged with sabotage and conspiracy to overthrow the government. From the beginning of the trial—which came to be known as the Rivonia Trial—the men knew they faced the very real possibility of the death sentence. Because the government already had evidence indicating their guilt, the men decided not to deny their involvement in acts of sabotage. Instead, they would use the trial to make a case against the state and its unjust laws. In a four-hour speech that gained international acclaim,

No Appeal

Before the conclusion of the Rivonia Trial, Mandela and the other defendants told their lawyer they would not appeal, even if they were sentenced to death. They felt an appeal would weaken the stance they had taken in court—that they were willing to fight to the death for their freedom. Still, Mandela confessed he had no desire to become a **martyr.** But he reminded himself that even his death might "serve a useful purpose." He knew that if he and the other defendants were to be executed, their deaths would likely become a rallying point for the liberation movement.

DELA

OPPOSITE In a 1975 letter to his wife, Mandela commented, "the cell gives you the opportunity to look daily into your entire conduct, to overcome the bad and develop whatever is good in you."

Mandela told the court: "I have fought against white domination, and I have fought against black domination. I have cherished the ideal of a democratic and free society in which all persons live together in harmony and with equal opportunities. It is an ideal which I hope to live for and to achieve. But if needs be, it is an ideal for which I am prepared to die."

On June 11, 1964, the government found Mandela, Sisulu, and six of the others guilty. They were sentenced to life in prison. Still, the men were hopeful. They sensed that things were changing in their country and that one day they would walk free again. They just didn't know how long it would be until that day finally came.

From Prisoner to President

At Robben Island, a prison six miles (9.7 km) off the coast of Cape Town, the men lived in individual cells. The cells were small, with just enough room for a tall man like Mandela to lie down with his head against one wall and his feet against the other. Bedding consisted of a straw mat and thin blankets.

OPPOSITE: Following centuries of use as a prison, military base, and hospital, Robben Island was named a UNESCO World Heritage Site in 1999, thanks to its prolific political history.

The Afrikaner wardens demanded that the prisoners treat them as masters. For meals, the prisoners received cornmeal porridge or boiled corncobs. They spent their days using picks and shovels to mine lime from a quarry. Newspapers were forbidden, and the prisoners were allowed to write and receive only one letter every six months.

Still, the political prisoners didn't give up their convictions. They formed their own version of the ANC within prison, with Mandela as the head. They presented prisoners' complaints and organized strikes or work slow-downs in attempts to negotiate for more humane conditions. They saw their work within the prison as an extension of the larger struggle outside it.

Over time, conditions at the prison began to improve.

By 1966, the men were allowed to talk as they worked at the quarry. In 1977, manual labor ended altogether. The men were also allowed to take courses by mail, earning degrees in history, library science, politics, and other subjects. Over time, they began to receive censored news reports. Their quota of letters and visits also increased.

The growing contact with the outside world made Mandela aware of the movement for his freedom. Several countries had instituted economic **sanctions** against South Africa, demanding an end to apartheid. International pressure prompted the South African government to offer Mandela his freedom—if he would show public support for certain government policies. Mandela refused.

In March 1982, Mandela, Sisulu, and two other political prisoners were transferred to Pollsmoor Prison near Cape Town. There, they were allowed to receive

OPPOSITE Despite tragedies of apartheid's past, such as 1960's Sharpeville massacre (pictured), and its present 1980s streak of violence, Mandela was convinced the ANC should seek a more peaceful path forward.

more news of outside events, through both newspapers and visitors. Three years into his stay at Pollsmoor, Mandela was moved to his own cell. By then, violence had exploded across the country. ANC supporters carried out violent attacks on apartheid advocates, and the police responded with force. Mandela worried that both sides would suffer millions of deaths if something wasn't done soon. He decided it was time to open a dialogue with the government. He knew his colleagues in the ANC would likely disapprove. So he didn't tell them, reasoning that "there are times when a leader must move out ahead of the flock." In 1986, Mandela began secretly meeting with Minister of Justice **Kobie Coetsee**. He then sought and received the approval of the ANC's senior leadership.

In December 1988, Mandela was moved to Victor Verster Prison near Paarl, where he was given his own

TAKEAWAY

In 1986, Mandela began secretly meeting with Minister of Justice Kobie Coetsee. He then sought and received the approval of the ANC's senior leadership.

cottage within the prison compound. There, he could entertain visitors, including his family and members of the ANC. And he could continue to hold talks with the government in privacy.

In December 1989, Mandela met with South African president F. W. de Klerk. Two months later, on February 2, 1990, de Klerk announced the end of many apartheid restrictions. As he listened to the speech, Mandela was overwhelmed. "It was a breathtaking moment," he later wrote. "Our world had changed overnight."

Just over a week later, on February 11, 1990, Mandela was released. Hundreds of supporters gathered to watch him walk out the gates of Victor Verster Prison. As Mandela raised his clenched right fist in the ANC salute, the crowd roared. Though he was 71 years old, Mandela felt as if "my life was beginning anew."

For Mandela, that new life meant working harder than ever for the cause of liberation. He was elected deputy president of the ANC in 1990 and ANC president the next year. In interviews, Mandela stressed that he felt no bitterness toward his jailers. In prison, he had come to see how much blacks and whites had in common. Kind wardens had reaffirmed to him the "essential humanity" of all people.

Mandela continued to hold talks with de Klerk and other government officials. But even as they met, some of the worst violence in decades rocked the country. Although the ANC had halted its armed struggle, members of the party faced frequent attacks by the rival Inkatha Freedom Party—a **Zulu** antiapartheid group proposing less radical changes than the ANC. Government forces secretly supported Inkatha in its attacks.

In response, the ANC suspended talks with the government and held several nonviolent campaigns. But not everyone in the ANC was happy with this course. Some demanded that Mandela give them guns, not more talk about peace. Although Mandela had once supported violence, he told them, "The solution is peace, it is reconciliation, it is political tolerance." Mandela's commitment to solving the problems of his country peacefully was recognized with the 1993 Nobel Peace Prize, which he was awarded jointly with de Klerk.

Finally, on April 27, 1994, all the people of South Africa went to the polls. The ANC won more than 62 percent of the vote, making it the majority party in parliament (the governing body of South Africa). Parliament chose Mandela as the country's new president. He was inaugurated on May 10.

From the beginning of his presidency, Mandela made it clear that his goal was to "heal old wounds and build a new South Africa." First, he established the Truth and Reconciliation Commission (TRC), chaired by Archbishop Desmond Tutu. The TRC held hearings on the human rights abuses that had happened under

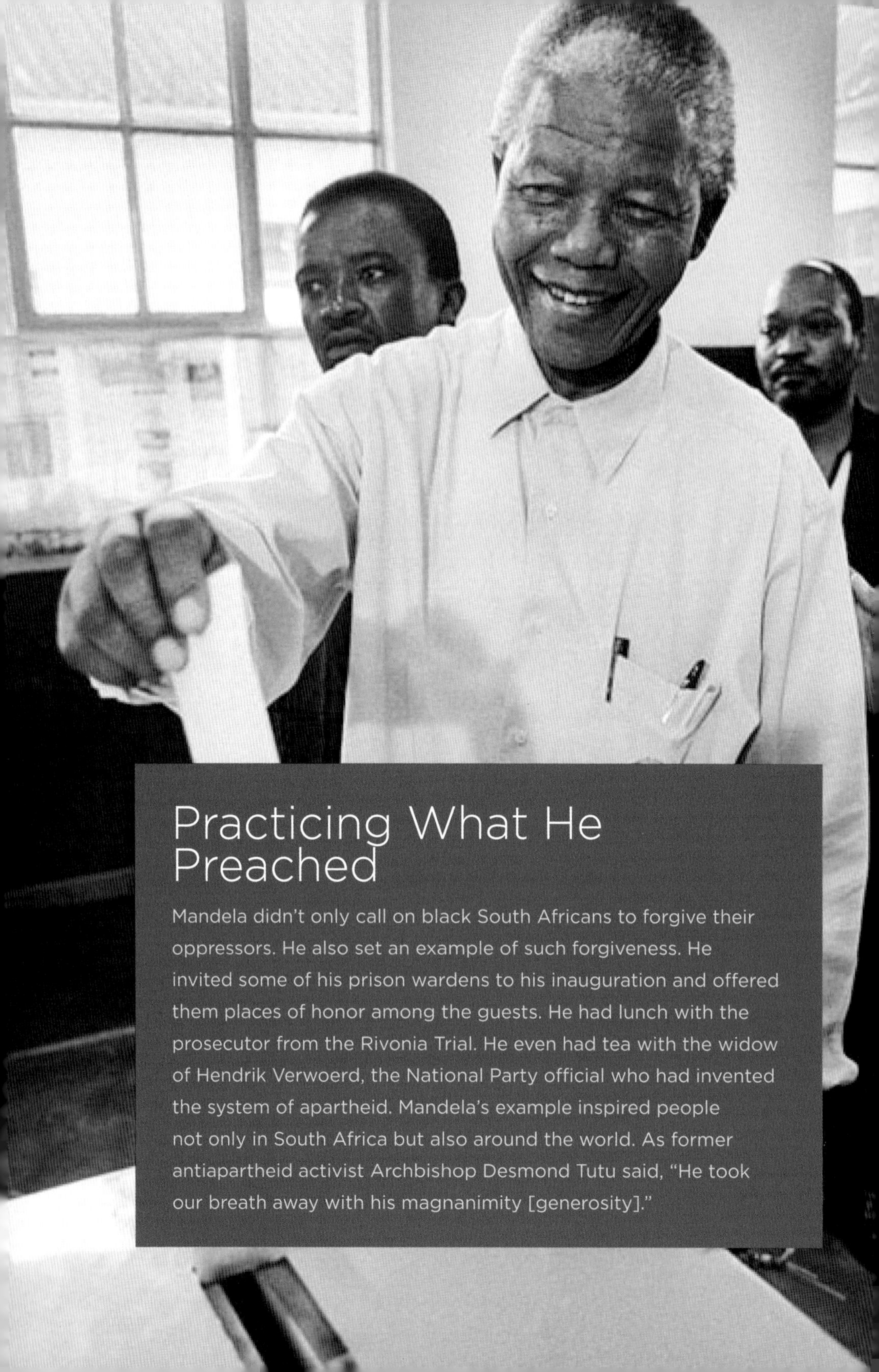

Practicing What He Preached

Mandela didn't only call on black South Africans to forgive their oppressors. He also set an example of such forgiveness. He invited some of his prison wardens to his inauguration and offered them places of honor among the guests. He had lunch with the prosecutor from the Rivonia Trial. He even had tea with the widow of Hendrik Verwoerd, the National Party official who had invented the system of apartheid. Mandela's example inspired people not only in South Africa but also around the world. As former antiapartheid activist Archbishop Desmond Tutu said, "He took our breath away with his magnanimity [generosity]."

Mandela believed the only way forward in the country was to acknowledge—and then forgive—past evils.

apartheid. Those who testified could apply for **amnesty**. Many black South Africans opposed Mandela's focus on reconciliation. But Mandela believed the only way forward in the country was to acknowledge—and then forgive—past evils.

Mandela also worked to improve living conditions for the country's black population. He established housing, education, and healthcare programs to improve the lives of the country's poorest citizens. Under his leadership, South Africa's economy began to grow again, although unemployment remained high.

Mandela had always made it clear he would serve

The Game That Changed South Africa

In 1995, South Africa hosted the Rugby World Cup. Before this, rugby in South Africa had been exclusively an Afrikaner sport. The South African rugby team's mascot, the springbok, was seen as a sign of apartheid. But Mandela realized the sport's potential to unite the country. Before the final game, Mandela walked onto the field wearing a Springbok jersey. The nearly all-white crowd cheered for their new president. Mandela's support united blacks behind the team as well. According to journalist John Carlin, the moment the team won the World Cup was the happiest in Mandela's political career. "It was the day his dreams came true," Carlin said.

OPPOSITE Among the thousands who attended Mandela's funeral were celebrities, heads of state, and fellow activists and humanitarians.

only one term as president. In 1999, he retired. He and Winnie had divorced in 1996, and in 1998, he had married Graça Machel. Now he looked forward to spending time with his new wife and his grandchildren in the home he had built in Qunu. But Mandela remained active. He became a leading advocate for HIV/AIDS education and continued to support causes of peace and human rights around the world.

Mandela died on December 5, 2013, at the age of 95. People of all races gathered to watch his funeral broadcast from Qunu. South African president **Jacob Zuma** pledged that Mandela would remain "our guiding light, illuminating the path as we continue the long journey to build the South Africa of [Mandela's] dreams."

QUOTE

"Never, never, and never again shall it be that this beautiful land will again experience the oppression of one by another and suffer the indignity of being the skunk of the world."

- Nelson Mandela, inauguration speech, May 10, 1994

From Life to Legacy

Realizing the South Africa of Mandela's dreams has proven harder than anticipated. According to sociologists Katherine Newman and Ariane De Lannoy, "Dramatic change was expected, if not overnight, then surely soon." But more than 20 years after Mandela's election to the presidency, many South Africans were still awaiting the promised changes. According

OPPOSITE: In 2015, more than half of South Africans lived in poverty, but such conditions disproportionately affected blacks and other people of color, as only 1 percent was white.

to Paul Oliphant, who participated in the antiapartheid movement, "We were expecting change. We were expecting to live together. But nothing changed at all."

Today, South Africa is among the richest countries on the African continent. It is also the most unequal in its distribution of wealth. Ten percent of the country's 54 million people hold 90 percent of the country's wealth. Most of them are white, although a small black middle class and a rich elite group have also formed. Some communities have been integrated, but many areas remain segregated by race and circumstance. Blacks simply can't afford to live in formerly "whites-only" areas of cities. Instead, many remain in townships on the edges of the cities. In many of these townships, people live in shacks made of zinc panels and wood scraps. Many do not have running water in their homes. In 2018, nearly 28 percent of the country was unemployed. The majority of those without jobs were black.

Although education is technically integrated as well, in practice most black students can't afford to enroll in good schools. Instead, some attend schools without desks or bathrooms. Overall, blacks receive fewer years of schooling than their white counterparts. Access to health care remains limited for most poor blacks as well, leading to a life span 16 years shorter than that of white South Africans. AIDS has ravaged many communities,

Family Regrets

Mandela frequently said his greatest regret was sacrificing time with his family to lead his country. From his earliest days in the ANC, he left home early and returned late at night, causing his young son to ask where he lived. In prison, Mandela spent decades separated from his loved ones. Afterward, he dedicated most of his time to the people of South Africa as their president. Reflecting on his life, Mandela said, "To be the father of a nation is a great honor, but to be the father of a family is a greater joy. But it was a joy I had far too little of."

leaving millions of children orphaned.

The continued inequality has led to rising racial tensions in South Africa. Some whites remain distrustful of the majority black government. They resent what they see as the government's favoritism of blacks through **affirmative action** programs in workplaces and universities. In some areas, racial tension has led to racially motivated violence against both blacks and whites. In 2016, South Africa's parliament introduced a controversial bill that would criminalize the use of racial slurs and hate speech.

In the face of such tension, many people in South Africa have begun to question the ability of the ANC to lead the country. In the years after Mandela left office—and especially after his death—the ANC was rocked by charges of corruption and a series of scandals. In 2017, protests erupted around the country calling for

In 2016, South Africa's parliament introduced a controversial bill that would criminalize the use of racial slurs and hate speech.

the resignation of president Jacob Zuma. He resigned on February 14, 2018. Zuma was replaced by **Cyril Ramaphosa**, who had served on Mandela's negotiating team as they ended apartheid. By 2018, Ramaphosa had become a successful businessman, with a net worth of more than $450 million. Some in South Africa questioned whether the former freedom fighter was still in touch with the average person of South Africa. Still, as he took office, Ramaphosa invoked the memory of the country's first black president: "Now is the time for all of us to work together, in honor of Nelson Mandela, to build a new, better South Africa for all."

Even as Ramaphosa pledged to continue Mandela's legacy, some South Africans began to question just what that legacy was. They blamed many of South Africa's current problems on Mandela's leadership—even before he became president. Some argued that Mandela's initial embrace of armed resistance was premature and that it led to many deaths as the state cracked down. Others said the focus on militancy pulled attention from other nonviolent measures that may have ended apartheid more quickly, if given a chance. Mandela's supporters, however, contended that without armed resistance, apartheid may have continued much longer.

Others pointed out that Mandela made mistakes as president. Although he promoted a free press, he frequently lashed out against black journalists who wrote critical pieces about the ANC. His loyalty to friends meant that he sometimes overlooked abuses of power. It also meant that he continued to offer support to Libya and Cuba—two countries that had supported the ANC—despite mounting evidence of the countries' human rights abuses against their citizens.

Mandela's economic policies have also been widely criticized. Many people said Mandela "sold out" to whites because he did not insist on transferring land and wealth from whites to blacks as the country transitioned to democracy. Although the majority black population was able to gain political power, they did not also gain economic power. As a result, nearly all the country's land—and wealth—remains in white hands. Even Mandela's best-known trait—his capacity for forgiveness—has been brought into question. According to journalist Alec Russell, "The otherworldly image of Mandela may have been what South Africa and the world wanted to believe, but great humanitarian as he was, he was always foremost a politician. Reconciliation was not a spontaneous miracle.... Rather, the seduction of the Afrikaners was carefully plotted in Mandela's cell, as a way to win and then retain power." Others agreed. Mandela's friend and biographer Anthony Sampson noted that though genuine, Mandela's acts of reconciliation and forgiveness were also a crucial part of his political strategy to "disarm" the Afrikaners.

One Good Thing about Prison

Mandela managed to find one good point about prison. "There is no prospect about prison which pleases—with the possible exception of one," he wrote in his autobiography. "One has time to think.... Prison provided the time—much more than enough time—to reflect on what one had done and not done." As Mandla Langa, a Mandela biographer, later explained, prison was essential to forming Mandela's ideas about the future of South Africa. "Prison, a place of punishment, instead became a place where he was able to find himself.... And it was, of course, in prison that his vision for rebuilding South Africa into a new democratic nation was born."

TAKEAWAY

In 2009, the United Nations established Mandela Day. The holiday is celebrated every year on Mandela's birthday, July 18.

Despite such statements, Mandela remains one of the most highly regarded humanitarians in history. His name has been given to streets, buildings, gardens, and schools around the world. Songs have been written about him, and his face has appeared on postage stamps. He's been honored with 126 honorary doctorates and 34 honorary citizenships. In 2009, the United Nations established Mandela Day. The holiday is celebrated every year on Mandela's birthday, July 18. On that day, people around the world are asked to spend 67 minutes doing humanitarian work—in honor of the 67 years Mandela spent fighting for freedom.

In his lifetime, Mandela was viewed as a terrorist by some and a liberator by others. Today, views of South Africa's first democratically elected president remain split. But no matter how they feel about Mandela, most South Africans acknowledge that they owe him for many of the freedoms they enjoy. He gave them the freedom to vote and to express their views, however critical those views were of him or of the government. Beyond that, Mandela became a symbol of what it meant to stand up to oppression and then to forgive the oppressor. At the time of his retirement, Mandela knew the struggle wasn't over. "The long walk continues!" he urged parliament. He trusted that his people—the united people of South Africa—would continue that walk into the future.

QUOTE

"There is a word in South Africa—*Ubuntu*—that describes [Mandela's] greatest gift: his recognition that we are all bound together in ways that can be invisible to the eye; that there is a oneness to humanity."

- Barack Obama, speech at Mandela memorial, December 10, 2013

Timeline

1918 Mandela is born July 18, in Mvezo, South Africa, a member of the royal line of the Thembu people of the Xhosa nation.

1930 Mandela's father dies, and Mandela goes to live at the Thembu royal palace, where he observes the leadership style of his guardian, Jongintaba Dalindyebo.

1939 Mandela enters the University College of Fort Hare but is eventually expelled for refusing a position on the student council.

1941 Mandela arrives in Johannesburg, where he finds work as a clerk in a law firm, eventually becoming a lawyer and opening the first black law firm in South Africa.

1948 The National Party wins South Africa's elections and soon institutes the system of apartheid.

1952 With the ANC, Mandela launches the Defiance Campaign to protest against apartheid; he is arrested for breaking curfew on June 26.

1956 Mandela and 155 other liberation movement leaders are arrested in December on charges of high treason.

1961 The Treason Trial ends on March 29, with all defendants found not guilty; afterward, Mandela goes underground and forms the militant organization MK.

1962 Mandela is arrested and found guilty of inciting a strike and leaving the country without a passport; he is sentenced to five years in prison on August 5.

1964 Following a police raid of MK headquarters, Mandela and other MK leaders are found guilty of sabotage and conspiracy and taken to Robben Island Prison on June 11 to serve a life sentence.

1986 Mandela begins secret meetings with government officials to work toward ending apartheid and establishing a new government.

1990 Mandela is released from prison on February 11.

1993 Mandela is awarded the Nobel Peace Prize jointly with South African president F. W. de Klerk.

1994 Mandela is inaugurated as South Africa's first black president on May 10.

1999 Mandela retires from the presidency after serving one term.

2013 Mandela dies on December 5, at the age of 95.

Selected Bibliography

Foster, Douglas. *After Mandela: The Struggle for Freedom in Post-Apartheid South Africa.* New York: Liveright, 2012.

Lodge, Tom. *Mandela: A Critical Life.* Oxford: Oxford University Press, 2006.

Mandela, Nelson. *Conversations with Myself.* New York: Farrar, Straus and Giroux, 2010.

Mandela, Nelson. *Long Walk to Freedom.* Boston: Little, Brown, 1994.

Mandela, Nelson, and Mandla Langa. *Dare Not Linger: The Presidential Years.* New York: Farrar, Straus and Giroux, 2017.

Newman, Katherine S., and Ariane De Lannoy. *After Freedom: The Rise of the Post-Apartheid Generation in Democratic South Africa.* Boston: Beacon Press, 2014.

Sampson, Anthony. *Mandela: The Authorized Biography*. New York: Alfred A. Knopf, 1999.

York, Geoffrey. "Mandela's Legacy: A Moral Beacon that Continues to Shine." *Globe and Mail.* Dec. 6, 2013. https://www.theglobeandmail.com/news/world/nelson-mandela/mandelas-legacy-a-moral-beacon-that-continues-to-shine/article15799688/.

Endnotes

affirmative action policy that seeks to make up for the effects of discrimination by ensuring the employment and education of certain groups, such as blacks or women

amnesty a government pardon or protection from prosecution for wrongdoing

apartheid South African system of laws that enforced segregation based on race

Cyril Ramaphosa South African lawyer and activist who lobbied for Mandela's release and served as chief negotiator in talks with the government; afterward, he went into business, becoming one of the nation's wealthiest men, before being elected president in 2018

Desmond Tutu archbishop in the Anglican Church whose nonviolent antiapartheid work was honored with a Noble Peace Prize in 1984

guerrilla type of warfare carried out by a small, often unofficial, army, often using tactics such as ambushes and surprise raids

Jacob Zuma South African activist who spent 10 years in prison on Robben Island before working for the ANC in exile and later serving as South African deputy president from 1999 to 2005 and president from 2009 to 2018, when he was forced to resign after several scandals

Kobie Coetsee South African minister of justice who initiated talks with Mandela; after Mandela's election as president, Coetsee served as president of South Africa's Senate

martyr a person killed for his or her beliefs

Oliver Tambo South African activist who opened a law firm with Mandela and later spent 30 years leading the ANC in exile from Lusaka, Zambia, before returning to South Africa in 1990

regent a person who rules on behalf of a king or other leader who is too young or sick or is otherwise unable to lead

sanctions measures, such as boycotts and trade bans, taken by the United Nations or by individual nations against a country that has violated international law to convince it to end the violation

Thembu Bantu-speaking people from eastern South Africa who make up part of the Xhosa nation

Walter Sisulu South African political activist who recruited Mandela into the ANC and was sentenced to life in prison with Mandela; he was released a few months before Mandela

Xhosa group of related peoples living mainly in eastern South Africa and consisting of several clans who speak related dialects of the Bantu language Xhosa

Zulu largest ethnic group in South Africa, made up of Bantu-speaking people from eastern South Africa

Websites

History: Nelson Mandela
https://www.history.com/topics/nelson-mandela

Learn more about Mandela's life and legacy through videos, pictures, speeches, and more.

Nelson Mandela Foundation
https://www.nelsonmandela.org/

The organization was founded by Mandela in 1999. It continues his work and shares his story with the world.

Note: Every effort has been made to ensure that any websites listed above were active at the time of publication. However, because of the nature of the Internet, it is impossible to guarantee that these sites will remain active indefinitely or that their contents will not be altered.

Index